DOING BUSINESS WITH GOD

AN EVERYDAY GUIDE TO PRAYER & JOURNALING

(Catrina J. Sparkman)

ISBN-13: 978-1-949958-03-4
Softcover 6x9 Edition

Doing Business with God: An Everyday Guide to Prayer & Journaling

Copyright © 2012 Catrina Sparkman

Published by The Ironer's Press

All rights reserved. No part of this book may be reproduced, stored in whole or in part, or transmitted in any form or by any means, without prior written permission from the publisher, except in the case of brief quotations embodied in articles for review. Nor can this book be circulated in any form of binding or cover other than that in which it is published.

All Bible Scriptures taken from the following translations: New International Standard Version, God's Word Translation, English Standard Version, and International Standard Version

Journal calligraphy featured on cover created by Wanda Tapp

Cover design & photography by P. Berkbigler Design & Illustration

ACKNOWLEDGEMENTS

To:

My mentor, Professor Sandra Adell, who, when I told her what I wanted to do, listened thoughtfully, and then gave wise counsel as to how to do it.

A Three Fold Chord, *A Place at the Table*, and the faithful warriors of *The Fourth Watch*, for your prayers, your tears, your laughter, your alms, and your unwavering support.

My children, Judah, Rain and Samuel, thank you for only complaining a little while mommy finished this book.

My mother, Patricia Thurman, for letting me order as many books from my grade school book order forms as I could possibly read. Just as you cared for and nourished me every day of my life, you fostered and encouraged an early love for reading in me that has never died.

My father, Cornell Thurman, who said to my mother, "Pat, explain to me why we are spending so much money on books?" Thank you for taking me to get my first library card, for paying all those overdue fines so that when I went to check out more books I would never be turned away, and for fostering in me a sense of frugality, and a love for the library system which also has never died.

My childhood pastor, Bishop Cheryl McBride Brown, for teaching me how to hear the Father's voice. This is unequivocally the greatest weapon I will ever have in my arsenal.

My adult pastors, Alex and Jackie Gee. Jackie, for inspiring me to stretch towards God's destiny for my life. Alex, for poking through the ashes of my dreams and saying, "Ms. Catrina I hear a heartbeat, this wants to live."

My husband, and best friend, Wesley Sparkman, who teaches me daily by his incredible patience, and faithful example, that it's not enough to know God's word, if you don't have the common sense to live it.

To all of you, I can't say it enough,

Thank you

DEDICATION

For Angela—a demand

TABLE OF CONTENTS

Author's Note i

Am I Even Qualified For the Job?.............................1

Getting Started 7

Search Me 13

Praise & Thanksgiving. 25

My Family 39

Enemies..53

The Church 67

The Lost 83

My Community...95

Government 107

Freestyle 119

Testimony 133

AUTHOR'S NOTE

I want to take a moment to personally thank you for purchasing your copy of *Doing Business with God: An Everyday Guide to Prayer & Journaling*. The greatest gift you could ever give anyone is the gift of prayer. Now, if you don't believe me, and you think I'm being overly spiritual right now, think for a moment about a person in the last stages of cancer, the one for whom the doctors have given up all hope. In the last moments of their lives, who do you think that person would rather have an audience with, a wealthy billionaire like Bill Gates or someone, who through prayer, knew how to touch the heart of Jesus?

> ಐಲ
>
> Satan wants to minimize the power of prayer in your mind so that you never understand the eternal damage your prayers do to his kingdom.
>
> ಐಲ

Beloved, as you become faithful in the ministry of prayer, you will learn how to touch the heart of Jesus. We've all heard this statement at one time or another: "All I can do is pray." Usually this is uttered by someone who feels like their back is up against a wall. They're standing at the foot of a colossal mountain for which they have neither skill nor talent to climb. What else is left for them to do but pray?

Those who know the power of God know that prayer is not a last resort; it's the first order of business. In fact, if I had to take a guess, I'd say it was Satan and his cronies who coined the phrase, "All I can do is pray." Why? Because Satan wants to minimize the power of prayer in your mind so that you never understand the eternal damage your prayers do to his kingdom.

> **Not praying about the lives God has given us stewardship over is like writing checks without looking at the balance in our checking accounts. Sooner or later we find ourselves powerless, morally and spiritually bankrupt.**

Touching the heart of Jesus, it's a captivating thought, right? That's essentially what Jesus was telling Martha when she fussed at Him about her sister, Mary. Martha, the one busy in the kitchen trying to prepare Jesus and His disciples something to eat, while her sister, Mary, sat attentively at the Master's feet. Jesus had this to say about Mary: "She has chosen the better portion and it will not be taken from her" (Luke 10:42). Martha had done a work for the kingdom that day too. She gave sustenance to the Creator's body. But Mary, just by merely spending time with Him, provided food for Jesus' soul. Mary touched God's heart. I can't help but think that something deep inside of Mary must have made her go against the pervading culture and convention assigned to the women of her day. Something whispering from the depth of her soul that said, "Mary, you're in the presence of greatness. Stop and memorialize this moment."

Like Martha, the culture and convention of today's society has many of us constantly on the go, from the moment our eyes pop open in the morning until the moment we fall back into comatose stupor at night. We want to be Mary, but . . . the bills, the children, promotion opportunities at work. Satan and his posse mass produce another lie, and suddenly we find ourselves entertaining the thought, 'I'm too busy to pray.' The reality is we're too busy not to pray. Not praying about the lives God has given us stewardship over is like writing checks without checking the balance in our bank accounts. Sooner or later we find ourselves powerless, morally and spiritually bankrupt.

> **Prayer & fasting were foundational pillars of the first church. If the church of today is to experience the power demonstrated by the first church these foundational pillars must return.**

Unless the Lord builds the house, the builders labor in vain. Unless the Lord watches over the city, the guards stand watch in vain. In vain you rise early and stay up late, toiling for food to eat—for he grants sleep to those he loves (Psalm 127:1-2).

In 2003, the Lord spoke to my heart concerning the ancient art of prayer and fasting. He said that prayer and fasting were foundational pillars of the first church, and if the church today wants to experience the power demonstrated by the first church in Acts, these foundational pillars must return. You do remember the first church in the Book of Acts, don't you? Where there was no need for a healthcare debate, because working class fishermen healed folks with their shadows; and the mantle of deliverance rested so heavily upon its members that actual prison doors, on more than one occasion, swung open (Acts 5:15, Acts 12:5-17, Acts 16:16-27).

Jesus seemed to be preparing His disciples for the reality of both prayer and fasting when they came to Him discouraged, no doubt, because they couldn't cast a demon out of a little boy. Jesus told His disciples, "This kind won't go out except by prayer and fasting." (Mark 9:29) We only need turn the television to the nightly news to see the ever increasing brokenness in our society. The kind of stuff that won't 'go out' except by prayer and fasting.

If my people, who are called by my name, will humble themselves and pray, and seek my face and turn from their wicked ways, then will I hear from heaven and will forgive their sin and will heal their land (2 Chronicles 7:14).

So as you begin this journey, let me impress upon you the great magnitude of what you are about to do. You are about to begin a dialogue with the Creator of the universe about this magnificent world He gave you. Welcome to *Doing Business with God*. I can't wait for you to hear what He has to tell you.

Sincerely,

Catrina J. Sparkman

Chapter One

AM I EVEN QUALIFIED FOR THE JOB?

What is prayer? Who can do it? Is there a certain skill set needed for the job? How do I even know if I'm called to this ministry? Maybe you've asked yourself one or all of these questions at some point or another. I know I certainly did when the Lord first impressed upon my heart to host Prayer Parties in my home in 2004. My conversation with the Holy Spirit went something like this:

"What in the world is a *Prayer party*?"
"It's like a Tupperware party except I'm pushing prayer, not plastic. And them who have no money are free to come and buy."
"But, Lord, surely you know my mom is the prayer warrior in the family, not me."
Silence.
"I don't have the slightest clue how to do any of this."
"Don't worry. I'll teach you."

Since then, I've learned that prayer can happen on the most ordinary days in the most ordinary ways. A prayer can be uttered in the words of a song, or tears when our hearts become too full. When no one else is there, God hears, and he counts our tears as liquid prayers.

One word, in a crisis—"Jesus"—is the most powerful prayer I've ever prayed. I remember calling on Jesus the very moment our car hit a deer traveling home from Milwaukee one weekend. As I

> The eyes of the Lord are combing across the earth, looking for someone, anyone, He can show Himself strong to.

screamed, "Jesus!" my husband and I watched the deer tuck its legs underneath its body and duck. The officer who took the report marveled at why the impact, which completely crumpled the front of our compact car, didn't cause the poor animal to fly onto the windshield and kill our family instantly. I, on the other hand, know exactly why. At the name of, Jesus, everything, including deer, must bow (Philippians 2:10).

Okay, okay, I can hear the most cynical among you saying, "Yeah, sure, for you maybe. You're the one writing the book. Obviously you've gotten over your fears and God has called you to this prayer thing. What about me? What if I don't necessarily feel the *prayer* call?"

Let's take a look at a well-known passage in the book of Ephesians. *So Christ himself gave the apostles, the prophets, the evangelists, the pastors and teachers, to equip his people for works of service, so that the body of Christ may be built up until we all reach unity in the faith and in the knowledge of the Son of God and become mature, attaining to the whole measure of the fullness of Christ* (Ephesians 4:11-13).

Please note that there is no official office of Intercessor listed here or anyplace else in scripture—at least not that I've found. Yet we know intercession is important to God, because He told us, on at least two separate occasions, that He was unhappy when no one took the job (Isaiah 59:15-16, Ezekiel 22:30). So, if there is no office of intercession, but God expects it to get done, who is He calling to do it? The answer is simple—everyone.

The eyes of the Lord, are combing across the earth, looking for people who are willing to cry out to Him. Looking for someone, anyone, He can show Himself strong to (2 Chronicles 16:9).

> **Prayer is both the responsibility and birthright of every human being. This is the blessing Adam experienced in the garden. We came out of Adam, so this is our inheritance too.**

I looked for a man among them who would build up the wall and stand before me in the gap on behalf of the land so I would not have to destroy it, but I found none (Ezekiel 22:30).

Pastors are called to pray. Teachers are called to pray. Apostles, prophets, and evangelists are called to pray. Senior citizens, deacons, ushers, strapping young men, and old men, young women, little children, dignitaries, kings, prostitutes, and government workers are all called to pray. Prayer is both the responsibility and birthright of every human being on the planet. It is a great privilege to talk to Elohim, our Creator God, and to have Him speak back to us. This is the blessing that Adam experienced in the Garden of Eden when he walked and talked with God in the cool of the day. And since we all came out of Adam, this is our inheritance too.

Scripture tells us that, at some point during these 'talks,' God brought the animals to Adam to see what he would name them (Genesis 2:19). Beloved, can't you see it, God setting up a co-partnership with man as it relates to this earth? "I'll make the animals and you name them." God is the same yesterday, today, and forever (Hebrews 13:8). He is still interested in hearing His people's thoughts about His earth. Heaven is His throne, earth is His footstool, but God will do nothing down here unless we pray.

I tell you with certainty, whatever you prohibit on earth will have been prohibited in heaven, and whatever you permit on earth will have been permitted in heaven (Matthew 18:18).

Let's just take a moment to *Selah*. This word, Selah, is used 74 times in the Bible. In scripture, whenever we read the word 'Selah', it means, take a moment and pause and think on whatever

> In the ultimate act of intercession, Jesus lived, bled, and died, so that we all might have access to the Father. The temple veil was torn from top to bottom. Now we all can wear the robe.

it is you just read. Right here, right now, let's take a moment and think about the state of the world today in connection with Mathew 18:18. Think about your city, your neighborhood, your local church, your community. Now think about your family—not just the people who live in your house, but extended family members as well. What, by the mere act of not praying, has been permitted to flourish?

You see, what I've discovered is that intercession isn't so much an office as it is a mantle. It's like the priestly robes worn by Aaron in the scriptures. When Aaron put on his robe, he was God's representative on earth doing business for and with God. When he took off the robe he was a regular everyday Joe. The difference between then and now is that Aaron couldn't just appoint himself priest. God had very strict rules about who could and could not approach Him in prayer, what the person could wear when they came into His presence, and how often they could come into His presence. These rules had to be followed down to the precise letter of His law, lest God in His Holiness accidentally killed somebody.

This awkward dance between lovesick Creator and sinful creation continued until Christ. The perfect Lamb without spot or wrinkle came to the earth as a man and bore in His body the penalty of humanity's sin. In the ultimate act of intercession, Jesus lived, bled, and died so that we all might have access to God the Father. The temple veil was torn from top to bottom and now we all can wear the robe. Think about that for a moment: because of the sacrifice of the Son, we all have access to the Father.

Jesus, speaking to His disciples before His death, told us all how to use our access pass after His resurrection. *In that day you will no longer ask me anything. Very truly, I tell you, my Father will give you whatever you ask in my name* (John 16:23). In prayer, we can place a hedge of protection around the people we love. We can plant godly things into the earth, and uproot the things God doesn't want to grow.

So, after you've thought long and hard about the Mathew 18:18 verse, pick up the mantle of intercession we talked about a few minutes ago. That's right, your robe. Now repent on behalf of your nation and your generation, repent on behalf of the church worldwide and your family. Oh, and about that skill set question you had earlier . . . settle it in your spirit today. If you are breathing and you have a pulse, you are qualified to do business with God.

SELAH NOTES

Chapter Two

GETTING STARTED

HOW TO USE THIS JOURNAL

This journal is divided into four main sections: **Search Me, Praise & Thanksgiving, Doing Business with God,** and **Testimony**. Each day as you sit down for prayer you will spend time journaling in each of these four sections. You will start in **Search Me** and move into **Praise & Thanksgiving.** From there you'll continue on into **Doing Business with God** which is divided into seven sub-categories: **Family, Church, Community, Enemies, The Lost, Government,** and **Freestyle.** I have divided the prayer targets into seven subcategories because there are seven days of the week. The goal is for you to spend time in prayer for one subcategory each day. When you get to the **Freestyle** subcategory, you'll do exactly what the name suggest: pray whatever is on your heart to pray.

There is nothing magical about the order of the sub- categories. You can choose to go down the list and start praying according to the day of the week, or you can come up with an order that is entirely your own. The main point is that you take one day of the week and pray for each sub-category. Example: On Monday pray for your family, on Tuesday the church, Wednesday the lost, Thursday your enemies, you get the picture. The last section you will visit in your time of prayer is **Testimony**. This is the place where you can record answers to your prayers or any promises or impressions God has laid on your heart.

How much time you spend in prayer is completely up to you. By just spending five minutes a day in each of the four sections, **Search Me, Praise & Thanksgiving, Doing Business with God, and Testimony,** you will have spent a very respectable twenty minutes a day in prayer. For someone who is moving from the Martha zone into the Mary zone, that is a wonderful start!

THE VALUE OF JOURNALING

How little or much journaling you do is totally up to you. You may choose to capture just the main idea of each prayer or you may choose to write out your thoughts in great detail. There is no right or wrong way to journal; it all depends on you. The idea behind journaling is to chronicle your time spent in prayer, to keep a written record of what you asked God in prayer and to become a keeper of the words God speaks back to you. God tells us in scripture how He feel about His Word: He honors His Word above all else (Psalm 138:2). Taking dictation from God helps us to learn how to honor His word. Another reason we journal is to see how far we've grown. Sometimes personal growth and development can appear to happen so slowly that it seems nonexistent. When we document our time with God, we can look back and be encouraged by the personal growth we see. So write legibly, because I promise you'll want to come back and read this later.

JUMP POINTS

Wherever it makes sense to do so, I've included what I call Jump Points after each section. I've included seven days', or seven weeks' worth of jump points (depending on what section you are in). The goal behind the Jump Points isn't to tell you what to pray, or even how to pray for that matter, but merely to give you some ideas about how to jump into your prayer time with the Father. Having said this, I realize that for many of you, prayer is second nature. If you feel like you can jump into the conversation with the Father without them, by all means, if that's you, go right ahead and jump! Just remember that for those days that you need an extra spark, the jump points are there to help you.

TIPS FOR SUCCESS

TIP #1: PLAN FOR PRAYER

Select a time each day that you will pray. Plan ahead. Put it on your schedule and add it to your day planner. Set a daily reminder on your cell phone until it automatically becomes part of your daily routine. Remember, whenever you take the time to plan for something, it increases the likelihood that you will actually do it.

TIP #2: START SMALL

It may be your heart's desire to meet God every day for an hour, but please understand that it takes time to become disciplined in prayer. We must learn how to practice the presence of God. If this is your first time making a daily commitment to prayer, or if you've had trouble with keeping your commitments in the past, start small. There's nothing wrong with starting small. Better to be faithful with a small amount of time than to set a large amount of time aside and not be faithful at all. Start off by setting aside 15 minutes a day for prayer. With a fifteen-minute-a-day plan, you could spend five minutes in the **Search Me**, five minutes in **Praise and Thanksgiving**, and five minutes praying in one of the daily sub-categories in **the Doing Business** section. You might not have very much to report when you first start praying, so it's alright if you skip the **Testimony** section at this stage. When you have been faithful to the daily commitment of 15 minutes for at least two weeks, bump your prayer time up to 20 minutes. When you experience success with 20 minutes a day, bump your prayer time up to 25 minutes.

> ෴
>
> Meeting God at the same time everyday helps you to become intentional about your gift of prayer. It also trains you to be respectful of God's time.
>
> ෴

By this time, you'll probably have some praise reports and answers to prayers to record, so start using the **Testimony** section. Continue adding time in five minute increments until you reach your end goal of where you want to be.

TIP #3: PRAY AT THE SAME TIME EVERYDAY

> *A trysting place is a personal open heaven whereby you and God abide. It's your set meeting space in the earth where the Creator steps into time to commune with you.*

Meeting God at the same time slot everyday will help you to do three things:

Number 1: *It helps you to become intentional about your gift of prayer*. When prayer is scheduled on your calendar and you have a reminder alert set on your phone, you mean business.

Number 2: *It trains you to be respectful of God's time*. By setting an appointment for prayer, you're saying, "God, I'd like to have an audience with you. Are you available at, say, 3 o'clock?" Now, when you make your appointment with Him, think about how you'd feel if you planned a lunch outing with a friend who then canceled on you at the last moment. Or, worse yet, she didn't even bother to call and cancel she just didn't show. Not only that but, after the first 'no show,' this same friend began to develop a pattern of not showing up. Most people, with even a few shreds of dignity would think, "Who in the world does she think she is?" And we're just mere mortals! What more would this kind of blatant disrespect feel like to a King?

Number 3: *It helps you carve out a trysting place for you and God*. What is a trysting place? I like to think of a trysting place as a personal open heaven whereby you and God abide. It's your set meeting space in the earth where the Creator steps into time to commune with you.

We know this is possible because scripture tells us that this very same thing transpired with Adam. We know that he and God had a set meeting place, 'the Garden,' and that Adam also had a time slot, 'the cool of the day.' If you faithfully keep your appointments with God, both you and He will begin to look forward to the time you spend together. After a while you will begin to feel His Spirit resting upon you at that time. That's God nudging you saying, 'I'm here now, let's pray.' This is the beginning of intimacy with God, and that's what this whole thing is about.

TIP #4: WHEN YOU FALL GET BACK UP

Now, perchance you don't make your time slot because, of course, life and the devil will fight you, still try your best to meet Him. Honor your commitment, but be courteous about it. Whisper a little note to God and let Him know, "Father, I'm sorry. I'm still coming, I'm just running a little late." And if you just can't make it to prayer at all, remember this: *A righteous man falls seven times but he gets back up* (Proverbs 24:16). When my children were learning how to walk and they fell down, as children inevitably will do, they would always look up at me to see what my reaction was going to be. If mama looked anxious or fearful in any way, that gave them permission to start screaming at the top of their little lungs. So I learned rather quickly to resist the impulse to wince, instead I would smile. "A righteous man falls seven times, but he gets back up," I'd say. They'd get up and dust themselves off and go on about their merry way.

Sometimes when we make a commitment to something and we don't hit the mark, we have a tendency to draw back, especially when we've made a commitment to God. Don't draw back. Get back up. "Lord, I know I said I would meet you and I didn't make it yesterday, but I'm sorry, and I'm here today." Don't let guilt, shame, defeat, or any other of Satan's buddies beat you up. Apologize with a sincere heart and move forward. God is making us into His image and likeness. He's perfecting us. He doesn't expect us to be perfect.

TIP #5: HAVE FUN

Talking to God about the things going on in your family, your community, and your nation is one of the most rewarding experiences you will ever have. Remember, a conversation is a two way street. You talk to Him, and He wants you to listen so that He can talk back. God never changes. He still longs to walk and talk with mankind just as He did with Adam in the cool of the day. So relax, enjoy Him, and allow Him to enjoy you.

Chapter Three

SEARCH ME

*Search me, O God, and
know my heart; test me and know my anxious thoughts.
See if there is any offensive way in me, and lead me in the way everlasting.*
Psalm 139:23-24

> ಸಂಡಿ
>
> Being in right standing with God and man, to the best of our ability, is an important first step to having our prayers heard on high.
>
> ಸಂಡಿ

This is the section where you quiet yourself before the Lord and ask Him to show you any areas of sin in your heart that need to be addressed. This step is so important to the Father that Jesus told us in Matthew 5:23 that if we are coming to do business with God, and we remember a problem between ourselves and another, we are to leave our gift and go make things right with that person. Then come back and offer the gift. Being in right standing with God and man, to the best of our ability, is an important first step to having our prayers heard on high. Now, that being said, there are times when reconciliation is just not possible. In those times God still expects us to keep our hearts swept clean on the matter. One of the benefits of meeting God daily in prayer is that you don't have the chance of building up offenses. We all sin and fall short daily, this is a fact. Starting your prayer time in **Search Me** allows you the opportunity to do a heart check.

> **We often think we know our true feelings but a better barometer of how we really feel is to listen to what comes out of our mouths about that topic. Out of the overflow of the heart the mouth speaks.**

Oftentimes, we think we know our hearts true feeling on a matter, but *the heart is deceitful above all things and beyond cure. Who can understand it?* (Jeremiah 17:9). A better barometer on how we feel is to listen to what we say on the matter. *Out of the overflow of the heart the mouth speaks* (Luke 6:45). In **Search Me** you are saying, "Lord, is there any hidden sin inside of me that doesn't please you? Is there any way that I have sinned or committed an offense against you?" Ask the Lord to show you any unforgiveness you may be harboring in your heart. Now stop, listen, and repent.

REPENT

Let's take a moment to talk about repentance. A commonly held misconception in Christian circles is that to repent means to say "I'm sorry. I apologize." When we repent, both regret and apology should be a part of the process, but these words alone don't express the true meaning behind repentance. The word *repent* means to change course, to turn from the path you were headed down and go a different way. We really repent before God, when we tell God, "I'm sorry, I won't do that again," and we make a conscious, sincere decision with both our heads and our hearts not to repeat the act again.

JUMP POINTS FOR SEARCH ME SECTION:

DAY 1- Start your prayer time by praying Psalm 51.

DAY 2- Meditate on Matthew 5:8. Ask God to show you anything in your heart that does not please Him.

DAY 3- Start your prayer time by reading Psalm 24. Ask God to show you any idols in your heart.

DAY 4- Ask for the blessing mentioned in Ezekiel 36:26.

DAY 5- Read and meditate on Psalm 78. Thank God for His mercy towards you.

DAY 6- Read and mediate on Proverbs 20. Ask the Lord to show you any un-forgiveness in your heart.

DAY 7- Meditate on Romans 12.

SEARCH ME GOD

SEARCH ME GOD

SEARCH ME GOD

SEARCH ME GOD

SEARCH ME GOD

SEARCH ME GOD

SEARCH ME GOD

SEARCH ME GOD

SEARCH ME GOD

Chapter Four

PRAISE & THANKSGIVING

Enter His gates with thanksgiving and His courts with praise; give thanks to Him and praise His name. Psalm 100:4

ಸಿಂಧ

Thanking God will get you inside His gates but praising Him will lead you into His courts. His court is the highest court in the land, and it is in His courts that your prayer petitions will be heard.

ಸಿಂಧ

Let's take a closer look at the above scripture in Psalm 100:4 and talk for a moment about the difference between praise and thanksgiving. The psalmist directs us to enter His gates with thanksgiving and to enter His court with praise. So what's the difference between praise and thanksgiving? Thanks is what we offer when someone does something for us. We thank them. This is just good old fashioned manners. It is polite to say thank you. Thank you requires no adoration or intimacy on our part whatsoever, just good home training. We thank people all day long—the cashier at the supermarket, the busboy at the restaurant, the police officer who could have given you a ticket but didn't.

Praise, on the other hand, is always personal, and it is always intimate. You cannot help but look up to and adore the one you praise. We thank God for what He has done, but we praise Him for who He is. So let's watch the progression. Thanking God will get you inside His gates. Praising Him will lead you into His courts. His court is the highest court in the land, and it is in this court that your prayer petition will be heard.

So in the *Praise & Thanksgiving* section, make sure to give Him both thanksgiving and praise. Bless God with the fruit of your lips. Thank Him for any truths He shows you about yourself in the *Search Me* section. Thank Him for being the God of Glory who answers prayer. Reflect on the magnificent fact that it is His Spirit that prays through you, and it is also His Spirit that will answer those prayers (Romans 8:26-27). He is truly the Intercessor and the Amen. The buck starts and ends with Him!

JUMP POINTS FOR PRAISE & THANKSGIVING:

DAY 1- Write a poem to the Lord about His goodness.

DAY 2- Read Psalm 117 and meditate on it. Think about a time when God has been good to you, and a time that He has shown His faithfulness to you.

DAY 3- Start your time by reading Colossians 3:16. Make up a new song to sing before the Lord.

DAY 4- Read Psalm 127 thank God for being the foundation that everything of worth is built upon in your life.

DAY 5-Read Psalm 147 and replace Israel and Jerusalem with your name and your family's name.

DAY 6- Write a love letter to God.

DAY 7- Thank the Lord for His promises outlined in Zephaniah 3:17.

PRAISE & THANKSGIVING

PRAISE & THANKSGIVING

PRAISE & THANKSGIVING

PRAISE & THANKSGIVING

PRAISE & THANKSGIVING

PRAISE & THANKSGIVING

PRAISE & THANKSGIVING

PRAISE & THANKSGIVING

PRAISE & THANKSGIVING

PRAISE & THANKSGIVING

PRAISE & THANKSGIVING

DOING BUSINESS WITH GOD

I no longer call you servants, because a servant does not know his master's business. Instead, I have called you friends, for everything that I learned from my Father I have made known to you. John 15:15

ଚଠ

Spirit led prayer is hearing the heart of Jesus and then praying His heart into the earth.

ଚଠ

Spirit led prayer is first hearing the heart of Jesus, then praying His heart back into the earth. Now that you have spent time in the *Search Me* and *Praise & Thanksgiving* sections, you are ready to do just that. Now it's time to hear the Lord's heart concerning your **Family, your Enemies, your Community, The Lost, The Church, Government** and whatever else He puts on your heart in the **Freestyle** section. Choose one sub-category for each day of the week and spend time journaling your prayers in that section.

Chapter Five

FAMILY

Behold, how good and pleasant it is when brothers live together in unity. It is like precious oil poured on the head, running down on the beard, running down on Aaron's beard, down upon the collar of his robes. It is as if the dew of Hermon were falling on Mount Zion. For there the Lord bestows his blessing, even life forevermore. Psalm 133:1

Unity in families, this really is the heart of God. The writer in Psalm 133 says unity among brothers is like the fragrant oil that dripped down onto the robes of the ancient Hebrew priests. The power behind this analogy is that the same priestly garment would be passed down from one generation to the next. When the son came of age and took up his priestly office, he would be anointed with the precious oil. It would be poured on his head just as it had been poured on his father's head during his ordination service before him. The oil would run down the son's beard and face, just like it had run down his forefathers' faces before him; just like it had run down the face of the first priest in that family, Aaron. This one robe would be stained with generations of anointing oil. And it would be a sign to that family, forever, that Yahweh is a God who cuts covenants with families.

ఐఠ

Our life spans are too short for the Eternal God, when He cuts covenant with us, He cuts covenant with everything and everyone in us. He is a God of the generations.

ఐఠ

Our life spans are too short for the Eternal God; when He cuts covenant with us, He cuts covenant with everything and everyone inside of us. He is a God of the generations.

This is the section where you ask yourself the question, "How is my family really doing?" Who is thriving, and who is hanging on by a thread? Is your family a strong unit, or is there fighting and dissention among you? Is there anyone in your family in bondage to any form of substance abuse? Are there orphans and widows among you? How are the marriages in your family doing, really? What about the next generation, how are the children? If you are married don't forget to also lift up prayers and petitions for your in-laws. Is there anyone in your family who doesn't know the love of Jesus? If any member of your family were to close their eyes in eternal rest tonight, could you be absolutely sure where they would spend eternity?

1 Peter 3:1 tells us that a wise woman can win her unsaved husband without ever speaking a word to him. It's obvious to me that this woman is a woman of prayer, and she's smart too. She knows how to keep peace in her home.

Sometimes we think that the only way to win our families for Christ is to preach them in into the kingdom. Many times this approach backfires and we end up doing more harm than good. As relatives are quick to tell you, they knew you when you weren't a Christian. They remember that time when . . . well, I'm sure you have your own story blank that you can fill in. So let's try the wise woman of 1 Peter's approach. Pray your family into the kingdom, and as you make intercession for that one in your family that seems like the most hopeless of causes, remember that our God, Yahweh, is a God of families.

JUMP POINTS FOR PRAYING FOR YOUR FAMILY:

WEEK 1: Meditate on 1 Timothy 5 and 1 Corinthians 13. Pray for real love, and charity to abound in your family. Ask God to show you practical ways to be a blessing to family members.

WEEK 2: Read Acts 16:16-34. Stand on the promise Paul made the jailer as you pray for your family, "If you believe on the Lord Jesus, you and your whole household will be saved."

WEEK 3: Read Numbers 35:9-21 and Ephesians 6:10-18. Our battle is not against flesh and blood, so what spiritual enemies are attacking your family members today?

WEEK 4: Start your prayer time by meditating on Malachi 4, Matthew 18:1-7, and Psalm 127. Pray for the children in your family, come against the negative influence of the culture on their lives. Pray also that they would be protected from predators.

WEEK 5: Read Genesis 2:24, and Ephesians chapter 5. Pray for marriages in your family.

WEEK 6: Read Acts 2, pray that God's spirit of revival would be poured out on your family.

WEEK 7: Read Joshua 24:1-15. Joshua starts by recalling Israel's history with God. He ends by renewing his family's covenant to serve God. Write a brief account of your family's history with God. Renew your covenant with God on behalf of your family.

PRAYERS FOR MY FAMILY

PRAYERS FOR MY FAMILY

PRAYERS FOR MY FAMILY

PRAYERS FOR MY FAMILY

PRAYERS FOR MY FAMILY

PRAYERS FOR MY FAMILY

PRAYERS FOR MY FAMILY

PRAYERS FOR MY FAMILY

PRAYERS FOR MY FAMILY

PRAYERS FOR MY FAMILY

PRAYERS FOR MY FAMILY

Chapter Six

MY ENEMIES

But I tell you who hear me: Love your enemies, do good to those who hate you, bless those who curse you, pray for those who mistreat you.
Luke 6:27-29

This is the section where you will lift up those who have hurt or offended you. Even the most peaceful among us find ourselves at odds with people sometimes. This section includes people who you may not necessarily consider enemies—maybe enemy is too harsh of a word. But you do find it difficult to love or relate to them. Perhaps you're in a place where you couldn't speak a kind word to that person if you tried, or speak well of them if their name came up in a conversation. I can tell you from experience that as you began to call their names before the Father in prayer, you will find your heart softening towards them.

Spending intentional, dedicated time in prayer for our enemies is one of the best ways to keep our hearts free of bitterness. Let the Holy Spirit lead you. You'll be amazed at how the Holy Spirit inspires you to pray for your enemies and how empowered you will walk away from your prayer time feeling.

> **Spending intentional, dedicated time in prayer for our enemies is one of the best ways to keep our hearts free of bitterness.**

PLANTING THE TREE OF FORGIVENESS:

Working in the ministry of healing and deliverance has taught me that in God's economy, harboring un-forgiveness in our hearts is an absolute 'no-no'. The God of Glory will not abide the hypocrisy of un-forgiveness when He has forgiven us so much. There have been times when myself and certain ministers on my team have been in a counseling session with someone, and it became clear that God would not grant them the healing they so desperately wanted, and the healing God so desperately wanted for them to have, until they first let go of anger and un-forgiveness. The moment the person makes the decision to forgive, God's healing waters floods their mind, body and soul.

What I have learned through my own experiences, as well as from helping others walk through their deliverance, has forever altered my prospective on the subject of forgiveness. I have learned that forgiveness is a tree that has to grow up. After you've made the decision to forgive, I mean really forgive, you feel better about it initially. You might cry, release some pent up emotions. You repent for harboring bitterness in your heart, and the love of God seems to permeate your entire soul—initially. But then another incident happens, often with that same person, and all of a sudden that warm fuzzy feeling you had when you first made the commitment to forgive with all your heart, well . . . you can't explain it, but, it's just not there anymore. You find yourself wondering, 'Did I ever truly forgive in the first

> **In God's economy, harboring un-forgiveness in our hearts is an absolute 'no-no'. The God of Glory will not abide the hypocrisy of un-forgiveness when He has forgiven us so much.**

place?' But here's what really happened. When you made the decision to forgive, you dug a hole in the ground and you planted a small tree in the spirit. I mean a really, really, really small tree. This tree needs a lot of water, attention, and love.

True biblical forgiveness is probably one of the hardest principles we will ever have to master. Even the disciples asked, Jesus, "How many times should we forgive our brothers? Lord, what about seven times? How does that sound?" They said seven, no doubt, because seven is a number in Scriptures that represents spiritual completion. In their minds they were probably thinking that if you wrong me seven times and I forgive you each one of those seven times, I must be a real disciple of Jesus, right? But no, Jesus' response to them was to forgive seven times seventy times. Seven times seventy times? Seriously, Jesus, by the time you forgive that much you've lost count of when you can legally walk away. And that's the whole point. God wants us to lose count. I think what Jesus was saying to the disciples was this: forgiveness is a tree that has to grow up. Keep watering it. Forgive until the act of forgiveness is rooted deep down inside of you.

> **When you made the decision in your heart to forgive, you dug a hole in the unseen realm, and planted a small tree called forgiveness. This tree needs a lot of water, attention, and love in order to grow.**

Every time we pray for someone who has hurt or offended us, we are cultivating the tree of forgiveness. Every time we bless them and not curse them, we are watering the tree of forgiveness. We are acting out the very meaning of forgiveness. You can't hate someone you are constantly praying for. It's impossible; I've tried it, and I invite you to try it too. Keep praying for your enemies until the tree of forgiveness is fully grown. How do you know when the tree of forgiveness is fully grown? Well, when it doesn't hurt anymore, when the sound of that person's name or the sight of their face doesn't cause you to cringe in your soul. When the leaves have grown so large in your heart that they block out the details of that awful thing that was done to you, that memory that keeps reverberating in your head—that's when you know the tree is full grown.

As I write this, I realize that some who are reading this have gone through unthinkable ordeals and atrocities. Things that no human being, no child, no woman, no man, should ever have to bear. My intention in writing this is not to minimize your pain but to comfort you and to emphasis God's ability to heal to the uttermost.

This is the same God who delivered three Hebrew boys who wouldn't bow down to Nebuchadnezzar from a fiery furnace (Daniel 3). Scripture tells us that when God delivered them, no harm had been done to their bodies, their hair was not singed, and the smell of smoke wasn't in their clothes. How is that even possible? You can burn a bag of popcorn in the microwave and the smell takes hours to dissipate from a room. How can God erase the very smell, the very taste, the very memory of that thing? The answer is simple, beloved: He's God.

You may think the painful memories will never go away, but I'm here to tell you that our God wants to heal you to the uttermost. Plant the tree of forgiveness. Water it with often with prayers and declarations of blessing over your enemies and you will reap a righteous harvest.

JUMP POINTS FOR PRAYING FOR ENEMIES:

WEEK 1: Read Proverbs 24. Pray for your enemies as the Holy Spirit leads you.

WEEK 2: Read Romans 12. Pray for your enemies as the Holy Spirit leads you.

WEEK 3: Read Psalm 57. Pray for your enemies as the Holy Spirit leads you.

WEEK 4: Read Psalm 25. Pray for your enemies as the Holy Spirit leads you.

WEEK 5: Read Matthew 26. Think of all the ways Jesus was betrayed. Ask the Lord to give you His heart for your enemies.

WEEK 6: Pray Psalm 37. Pray for your enemies as the Holy Spirit leads you.

WEEK 7: Meditate on Luke chapter 6. Pray for your enemies as the Holy Spirit leads you.

PRAYERS FOR MY ENEMIES

PRAYERS FOR MY ENEMIES

PRAYERS FOR MY ENEMIES

....
....
....
....
....
....
....
....
....
....
....
....
....
....
....
....
....

PRAYERS FOR MY ENEMIES

PRAYERS FOR MY ENEMIES

PRAYERS FOR MY ENEMIES

PRAYERS FOR MY ENEMIES

PRAYERS FOR MY ENEMIES

PRAYERS FOR MY ENEMIES

Chapter Seven

THE CHURCH

Now this is what the Lord Almighty says: "Give careful thought to your ways. You have planted much but have harvested little. You eat, but never have enough; you drink but never have your fill. You put on clothes, but are not warm. You earn wages, only to put them in a purse with holes in it. This is what the LORD Almighty says: "Give careful thought to your ways. Go up into the mountains and bring down timber and build the house, so that I may take pleasure in it and be honored," says the LORD. You expected much but see, it turned out to be little. What you brought home blew away. Why? Declares the Lord Almighty, "Because of my house which remains a ruin, while each of you is busy with his own house. Therefore, because of you the heavens have withheld their dew and the earth its crops. I called for a drought on the fields and the mountains, on the grain, the new wine, the oil and whatever the ground produces, on men and cattle, and the labor of your hands.
Haggai 1: 5-11

> **Today when God talks about His church, He's not talking about buildings made of mortar and stone, but living temples made up of bones, flesh, breath and sinew.**

Somewhere around 520 BC, Haggai spoke this prophetic word to the recently returned Jewish exiles. They had been in captivity in Babylonian territory for 70 years and when they were finally given permission to return to their homeland, the first thing they did was set to work rebuilding God's temple. It took two years to complete the foundation, and after they were finished, they had a great celebration. But, like anyone who ever tries to build anything for God, these Jews met opposition, mostly from their Gentile neighbors who feared the social, political, and no doubt spiritual implications of a rebuilt temple at the heart of a thriving Jewish state. Long story short, the naysayers where able to make enough noise, apply enough pressure, and provide enough red tape that the building process was halted for the next sixteen years. It is under these circumstances that Haggai brings them this word from the Lord, "Get back up and build." But the Spirit of God was saying something else to His people: "This isn't just about you, the earth is waiting for this."

There is something about God's church being 'built up' that causes the land to flourish. God's church should carry the kind of spiritual muscle that shifts atmospheres and regions, the kind of clout that causes the heavens to drop their dew and crops to grow. The church should have the type of authority that causes social and economic prosperity to enter a region just because the people of God are there. Where there is a strong, active church in a community, the people of that community should prosper.

God expected this to be true for the returned exiles and He expects it to true for the body of Christ today. Only today when God talks about His church, He's not talking about a building made of mortar and stone. He is talking about living temples made of bones, flesh, breath, and sinew. To build God's church means to build his people.

As you pray in this section, consider the state of your local church fellowship. Is there economic vitality in the city where you live because your church is there? Has the crime rate dropped in your area because the church of God and His people are there? If the answer to these questions is not

ఐఆ

God's church should carry the kind of spiritual muscle that shifts atmospheres and regions, the kind that causes the heavens to drop dew and social and economic prosperity to enter an area just because the people of God are there.

ఐఆ

an unequivocal "yes," don't stop praying until it gets there. As you lift up the needs of your local church, remember that Jesus is coming back for one unified church. He won't be picking up the Catholics on Monday, the Protestants and Baptists on Tuesday, the Lutherans on Saturday . . . well, I don't need to belabor that point. Although the body of Christ is segmented by denominations and church affiliations, I encourage you to see the body of Christ as one. When you lay before the Lord in prayer for the church, don't just offer up petitions for your local house of worship and your pastor. Offer up petitions for pastors and ministers everywhere in houses of God throughout your country and throughout the world. In doing so you will be praying like Jesus prayed, that we all might be one even as He and the Father are one (John 17:21).

JUMP POINTS FOR PRAYING FOR THE CHURCH

WEEK 1: Read and meditate on Revelation 2:2-7. Pray that the church worldwide would return to Jesus, her first love.

WEEK 2: Read and meditate on Revelation 2:8-11. Pray for the persecuted church all over the world.

WEEK 3: Read and meditate on Revelation 2:12-17. Pray that the church would not be conformed to the culture of the world, but that the church would begin to define and influence modern day culture.

WEEK 4: Read and meditate on Revelation 2:18-29. As you pray for the church worldwide pray against a religious spirit, the very spirit that killed Christ. Pray that the true worshipers would arise, those that worship God in Spirit and in truth.

WEEK 5: Read and mediate on Revelation 3:1-6. Pray that God's Spirit of revival would fall upon the church. Pray for those who are spiritually dead in the body of Christ today.

WEEK 6: Read and meditate on Revelation 3:8-13. Pray for those who are weak and tired in the body of Christ today. Pray that their faith would not waver. Ask God to send reinforcements to them in the form of ministering angels to encamp around them and give them courage and strength.

WEEK 7: Read and meditate on Revelation 3:14-22. Pray that a spirit of repentance would fall upon the church worldwide.

MY PRAYERS FOR THE CHURCH

MY PRAYERS FOR THE CHURCH

MY PRAYERS FOR THE CHURCH

MY PRAYERS FOR THE CHURCH

MY PRAYERS FOR THE CHURCH

MY PRAYERS FOR THE CHURCH

MY PRAYERS FOR THE CHURCH

MY PRAYERS FOR THE CHURCH

MY PRAYERS FOR THE CHURCH

MY PRAYERS FOR THE CHURCH

MY PRAYERS FOR THE CHURCH

MY PRAYERS FOR THE CHURCH

Chapter Eight

THE LOST

One day as Jesus was standing by the Lake of Gennesaret, with the people crowding around him and listening to the word of God, he saw at the water's edge two boats, left there by the fishermen, who were washing their nets. He got into one of the boats, the one belonging to Simon, and asked him to pull out a little from shore. Then he sat down and taught the people from the boat. When he had finished speaking, he said to Simon, "Pull out into deep water, and let down the nets for a catch." Simon answered, "Master, we've worked hard all night and haven't caught anything. But because you say so, I will let down the nets." When they had done so, they caught such a large number of fish that their nets began to break. So they signaled their partners in the other boat to come and help them, and they came and filled both boats so full that they began to sink. When Simon Peter saw this, he fell at Jesus' knees and said, "Go away from me, Lord; I am a sinful man!" For he and all his companions were astonished at the catch of fish they had taken, and so were James and John, the sons of Zebedee, Simon's partners. Then Jesus said to Simon, "Don't be afraid; from now on you will catch men." So they pulled their boats up on shore, left everything and followed him.

Luke 5:1-11

> We are all called to be fishers of men, to fulfill the great commission and to lead others to Christ. One of the easiest ways to do this is through prayer.

It is certainly no coincidence that the first disciples were fishermen by trade. We are all called to fulfill the great commission to lead others to Christ. We are all called to be fishers of men. One of the best and easiest ways to do that is to remember the lost during your time of prayer. As you pray for the lost, I want to encourage you, like Jesus encouraged Peter, to stretch your faith wide in this area. Take this as far as you are willing to believe. Ask God for the salvation of your entire neighborhood, the company where you work, ask Him to save the politicians over your city. As you are riding in your car, ask God to save everyone on the road where your tires tread. If there be any unsaved that travel along your path, claim them for the kingdom. Remember, God is willing to answer any prayer that is prayed in accordance to His will (1 John 5:14). So you can pray with great vigor for the lost because you already know God's will on the matter. It is His will that none should perish (2 Peter 3:9). So step out in faith and launch your boat out into the deep and let down your prayer nets. So that when you close your eyes in this life and wake up in eternity the Father can look at you and say, "Well done, my good and faithful servant, enter into my rest." And when He points to the multitudes behind Him, He can also say, all of these came into the kingdom, because you prayed.

JUMP POINTS FOR PRAYING FOR THE LOST

WEEK 1: Start your prayer time by reading and meditating on John 4:1-38. Jesus went to Samaria, a town where, if they could help it, Jews rarely traveled. Clearly the Savior of the world wanted to have a personal encounter with the women at the well. Pray for the broken and destitute today. Ask Jesus to give His living water to them, just as He gave it to the Samarian woman He met at the well.

WEEK 2: Start your prayer time by reading and meditating on Luke 15. As you pray, think about the importance of just one life to God. If only one person would have received the gift of salvation, Jesus would have still died on the cross. Worship Him in your prayer time today.

WEEK 3: Start your prayer time by reading and meditating on Acts 2. Just like God poured out His Spirit at Pentecost, ask Him for another great outpouring of His Spirit, so that a great harvest of souls can come into the kingdom.

WEEK 4: Start your prayer time by reading and meditating on John 11. In verse 43, Jesus stood outside of Lazarus' tomb and told the dead man to, "come forth." Jesus said that those who followed after Him would do even greater work than He did. So as you pray for those who are the spiritual dead, see yourself standing outside their tombs. In the name of Jesus, command them to come forth.

WEEK 5: Start your prayer time by reading and meditating on John 3 and 2 Timothy 3. Pray for the lost inside the church today. Pray for all those who have religion but no real relationship with Jesus.

WEEK 6: Start your prayer time by reading and meditating on Luke 5: 1-11. Ask God to help you fulfill the great commission. Ask Him to make you a fisher of men.

WEEK 7: Start your prayer time by reading and meditating on Luke 12. Pray for the greedy today. Also pray for those who are rich in earthly possessions but are poor and impoverished in spirit. Pray that they would come into the kingdom.

MY PRAYERS FOR THE LOST

....
....
....
....
....
....
....
....
....
....
....
....
....
....
....
....
....

MY PRAYERS FOR THE LOST

MY PRAYERS FOR THE LOST

MY PRAYERS FOR THE LOST

MY PRAYERS FOR THE LOST

MY PRAYERS FOR THE LOST

MY PRAYERS FOR THE LOST

MY PRAYERS FOR THE LOST

MY PRAYERS FOR THE LOST

Chapter Nine

MY COMMUNITY

You are the salt of the earth, but if salt has lost its taste, how shall its saltiness be restored? It is no longer good for anything except to be thrown out and trampled under people's feet. You are the light of the world. A city set on a hill cannot be hidden. Nor do people light a lamp and put it under a basket, but on a stand, and it gives light to all in the house. In the same way, let your light shine before others so that they may see your good works and give glory to your Father who is in heaven.
Matthew 5: 13-16

> **As you pray for the people who make up your world, remember that for some of them, the only connection to the Living God they will ever have is through you.**

This is the section where you lift up the needs and concerns of your community. We all have multiple communities we belong to, whether they be the people who make up our church fellowships, the people in our neighborhoods, the co-workers on our jobs, or the different athletic, civic and social clubs we participate in. You may also see your community as a particular ethnic or racial group with which you share a common experience or heritage. Whoever and whatever you define your community to be, this is where you would lift up those needs.

The Bible declares that as iron sharpens iron, so does a friend sharpen a friend (Proverbs 27:17). And as I stated earlier, the best thing you can ever do for anyone, especially a friend, is to call their names in prayer. Pray for their destiny, for their choices, their walk with God. Lift up their families. As you pray for the people who make up your world, remember that for some of them, the only connection to the Living God they will ever have is through you. Ask the Father where and how He would have you to pinpoint those prayers. Remember, He is always looking for an intercessor to stand in the gap and pray for those who cannot reach heaven for themselves, so He is more than willing to help you.

JUMP POINTS FOR PRAYING FOR THE COMMUNITY:

WEEK 1: Start your prayer time in this section by reading Luke 10:25-37. Ask God to show you practical ways you can be a blessing to someone in your community.

WEEK 2: Start your prayer time in this section by reading Galatians 6:1-10. Ask God to show you the burdens of your community as you pray. Bring those problems before the Lord in prayer.

WEEK 3: Start your prayer time by reading Jeremiah 5. Go on a prayer walk through your neighborhood and take an honest inventory of your community just as Jeremiah had to take an honest inventory of his community. Bring the things you see or sense before the Father in prayer.

WEEK 4: Start your prayer time in this section by reading Ecclesiastes 4. Pray for the oppressed in your community.

WEEK 5: Start your prayer time by reading Matthew 22:37-40. Ask the Lord to show you tangible ways you can show love to your neighbor.

WEEK 6: Start your prayer time in this section by reading John 15. Ask God to give you His heart for your community.

WEEK 7: Start your prayer time in this section by reading 1 Thessalonians 5. Pray for your community leaders. Pray that the will of God would be done in their lives.

PRAYERS FOR MY COMMUNITY

PRAYERS FOR MY COMMUNITY

PRAYERS FOR MY COMMUNITY

PRAYERS FOR MY COMMUNITY

PRAYERS FOR MY COMMUNITY

PRAYERS FOR MY COMMUNITY

PRAYERS FOR MY COMMUNITY

PRAYERS FOR MY COMMUNITY

PRAYERS FOR MY COMMUNITY

Chapter Ten

GOVERNMENT

First of all, then, I urge that entreaties and prayers, petitions and thanksgiving be made on behalf of all men, for kings and all who are in authority in order that we may lead a tranquil and quiet life in all godliness and dignity. 1Timothy 2: 1-2

In the **Government** section, you will lift up local, state, and national concerns. You may also be led to lift up international affairs as you read or hear about issues going on in other countries around the world. Some of you may be asking the question, right now, "Does God want Christians to be political?" This question has certainly come up in Christian circles before. To answer that question, let me redirect us back to the Matthew 18:18 verse: *I tell you with certainty, whatever you prohibit on earth will have been prohibited in heaven, and whatever you permit on earth will have been permitted in heaven.* You can't get much more political than that. And don't forget, the word of God instructs us to pray for the peace of Jerusalem (Psalm 122:6).

God's statement on government is rather short, simple, and to the point, but also rather profound. In the book of Timothy, He says pray for good government so that you can live a tranquil, quiet life that is godly and has dignity. It is not God's desire for

> ಸಿಂ
>
> **Whatever you prohibit on earth will have been prohibited in heaven, and whatever you permit on earth will have been permitted in heaven. You can't get much more political than that.**
>
> ಸಿಂ

> **Many Christians in the US get caught up in the sin of not praying for our leaders—especially if they didn't select them. These are US citizens who believe that God is a Republican or that God is a Democrat. The reality is God is neither; He's outside of our puny political system, and we each have a responsibility to pray across the aisle.**

His people to be oppressed. He doesn't want our dignity and our humanity stripped away from us. He doesn't want our freedom of worship and expression taken from us, and He certainly receives no pleasure when children around the globe grow up dodging bullets in war torn streets. He doesn't want this for any of His people.

So if you are a believer, and you are reading this book, and you live in a country where there is political unrest, I can say in all earnestness that this is not God's will for your nation because you live there. He is looking for somebody, anybody, who is willing to pray. Gather the believers in your city and begin to ask God for good government. You'll see a turn around when the people of God in your nation begin to pray.

Sadly, many Christians in the United States get caught up in the sin of not praying for our leaders once they have come to power—especially if they didn't select them. These are US citizens who believe with all their heart that God is a Republican, or that God is a Democrat. The reality is God is neither; He's outside of our puny political system, and we each have a responsibility to pray across the aisle.

I've also heard of Christians taking the position that, "Heaven is my home so I don't need to be concerned with what's going on down here." Neither of these positions is godly or biblical. The Bride of Christ, the church, is God's answer to a dying and broken world. If the church doesn't get involved in the political, who will provide the moral compass for our age?

The Church needs to raise her voice, to cast her vote in this realm, as well as in the courts of heaven. So if you live in a country where you are blessed enough to cast your ballot in a free election: do both. Vote and pray.

JUMP POINTS FOR GOVERNMENT

WEEK 1: Begin your prayer time for government by reading and meditating on Proverbs 21. Ask God for righteous government.

WEEK 2: Start your prayer time for government by reading Psalms 33. Ask the Lord to be the God of your nation.

WEEK 3: Start your prayer by reading Proverbs 8. Ask God for wisdom for your local, state, and national government.

WEEK 4: Start off your prayer time for government by reading and meditating on Proverbs 29. Pray for honesty in government and that all forms of corruption would be exposed.

WEEK 5: Begin you prayer time by reading and meditating on Isaiah 9:6-7. Pray that the greatness of God's government would come to your local government.

WEEK 6: Begin your prayer time by reading 1Timothy 2: 1-2. Pray for the children of God dispersed in cities all around the world. Pray that they would have good government and that they would be able to live quiet, peaceable lives.

WEEK 7: Begin your prayer time for government by reading Psalms 122. Pray for the safety of your own city, as well as the safety and peace of Jerusalem.

MY PRAYERS FOR GOVERNMENT

MY PRAYERS FOR GOVERNMENT

MY PRAYERS FOR GOVERNMENT

MY PRAYERS FOR GOVERNMENT

MY PRAYERS FOR GOVERNMENT

MY PRAYERS FOR GOVERNMENT

MY PRAYERS FOR GOVERNMENT

MY PRAYERS FOR GOVERNMENT

MY PRAYERS FOR GOVERNMENT

Chapter Eleven

FREESTYLE

And Elijah said to Ahab, "Go, eat and drink, for there is the sound of a heavy rain." So Ahab went off to eat and drink, but Elijah climbed to the top of Carmel, bent down to the ground and put his face between his knees. "Go and look toward the sea," he told his servant. And he went up and looked. "There is nothing there," he said. Seven times Elijah said, "Go back." The seventh time the servant reported, "A cloud as small as a man's hand is rising from the sea." So Elijah said, "Go and tell Ahab, 'Hitch up your chariot and go down before the rain stops you.'" Meanwhile, the sky grew black with clouds, the wind rose, a heavy rain came on and Ahab rode off to Jezreel. The power of the LORD came upon Elijah and, tucking his cloak into his belt, he ran ahead of Ahab all the way to Jezreel. 1Kings 18 41-45

This is a great story, and a powerful testimony of a human being doing business with the Almighty God. Elijah seems to come on the scene from out of nowhere. His very name means 'I worship Yahweh' in a time when Israel has become overrun and infested with the worship of Baal. Elijah presents himself before Ahab—the most wicked king in Israel's history—and tells him, "It ain't gonna rain until *I* say so." Talk about having spiritual muscle. Elijah said no rain, and for three and half years the heavens where shut—no rain, no dew, nada! All the water in Israel allocated for cattle has dried up, and King Ahab and his servant Obadiah are combing the land looking for blades of grass for the animals to chew in hopes of keeping the livestock alive for another day. These are the dire conditions the nation is in when the prophet Elijah presents himself before King Ahab again. This time, Elijah's conversation with Ahab goes like this: "Yeah, I'll bring back the rain, but some things are gonna have to change around here before I do."

Elijah has Ahab call a meeting on Mount Carmel were he challenges 450 prophets of Baal, and 400 false prophets of Asherah to a showdown. The rules of contest are simple, the god who answers by fire will be the national god and it will be illegal to worship any other god. The prophets of Baal and the prophets of Asherah cut themselves with swords and cry out to their god all day and late into the night. But since gods of stone and wood are both deaf and mute, Baal answered them back not a word. Elijah calls on the Living God and He answers immediately by sending down His fire. The people repent, and Elijah oversees the execution of the 850 false prophets. Now that the conditions for deliverance have been met, the rain can begin again. So Elijah gets down into a birthing posture, and he beseeches God for the rain.

> There is a realm we can go to in prayer where the people of God don't ask God for anything. He gives us His signet ring and, working in concert with Him, we declare a thing and what we declare shall be.

What's most interesting to me about this story is that God doesn't shut the heavens, a human does. Elijah seems to make an executive order and God sends His power and might to back up Elijah's decision. Beloved, there is a realm that we can enter in prayer, where the people of God don't ask God to give them what they are chasing after. God gives His people His signet ring. Working in concert with Him, they declare a thing and what they declare shall be. I call this the realm of declaratory grace, and I talk more about that in my upcoming book, *Territory*.

Elijah, operating in this realm of declaratory grace, looked around his nation and decided that something needed to be done. A wicked monarchy was in power who felt they didn't need to answer to anyone for their actions, least of all the Living God. The government needed to be reminded that in no uncertain terms, the earth is the Lord's and the fullness thereof (Psalm 24:1). Elijah was just the man to do it because Israel was his spiritual territory.

The heavens had been shut for three and a half years, but Elijah says, "I hear the sound of heavy rain." Well, how in the world did he hear that? Certainly nobody else heard it. Everybody else was preparing for the end. Elijah didn't hear the sound of rain with his natural ears, he heard by the spirit.

This is the section where you get to pray something new into the earth. Something that only you and God can hear and see. It may be a cure for Cancer or AIDS. It may be something that has been on your heart for a while, something you feel the Spirit nudging you to pray about. It may be a single issue or multiple topics that you need to lay on in prayer until you see breakthrough. The beauty of the **Freestyle** section is that you get to decide. You may choose to adopt a child, or a school, or a country, or people group in prayer. Let the Lord lead you. He will tell you what to pray, and when the season is up and when it's time to adopt a new project.

As you begin to pray for your project, you may even find God giving you more and more insight on the matter. You may feel the urging to research facts and statistics on your subject and know as much about it as you can. Don't forget to bring this information before the Father in prayer. Remember you are bringing your petitions before Him. His court is the highest court in the Universe. Any lawyer worth his or her salt would bring any factual evidence into the courtroom that would help to prove his or her case. You want to convince the King of Kings to rule in your favor, but you have the advantage that the lawyer in an earthly courtroom doesn't have: this Judge, although He is perfectly just, wants to rule in your favor.

JUMP POINTS FOR THE FREESTYLE SECTION:

WEEK 1: Start your time by reading Luke 18:1-8. As you knock on heaven's doors, be as persistent as the widow in Luke 18.

WEEK 2: Start your prayer time by reading Genesis 18. Pray with the understanding that God considers you. You have the ear of the Great Almighty King.

WEEK 3: Start your prayer time by reading Exodus 32. Pray with the understanding that you have favor with God. Your prayers hold sway in His court of justice.

WEEK 4: Start your time in this section by reading Mark 5: 21-34. Press your way into the Father's presence, just like the woman with the issue of blood pressed her way through the crowd to touch the hem of Jesus's garment.

WEEK: 5 Start your prayer time by reading Matthew 7. Pray with the confidence that you have a good Father in heaven who likes to give good gifts to those who ask Him.

WEEK 6: Read Luke 22:31-32, Job 1:1-12, Zechariah 3. Remember that Satan the Accuser comes before the throne of God to bring accusations against the people of God. As you pray, come against the accuser that is standing between you and 'the thing' or person you are praying for.

WEEK 7: Start your prayer time by reading and meditating on Hebrews 11. Pray with the knowledge and understanding that God specializes in the impossible. But it is impossible for you to have what you are asking if you don't believe. Ask God to strengthen your faith.

MY FREESTYLE PRAYERS

MY FREESTYLE PRAYERS

MY FREESTYLE PRAYERS

MY FREESTYLE PRAYERS

MY FREESTYLE PRAYERS

MY FREESTYLE PRAYERS

MY FREESTYLE PRAYERS

MY FREESTYLE PRAYERS

MY FREESTYLE PRAYERS

MY FREESTYLE PRAYERS

Chapter Twelve

TESTIMONY

My mouth will tell of Your righteous acts, of Your deeds of salvation all the day, for their number is past my knowledge. With the mighty deeds of the Lord God I will come; I will remind them of Your righteousness, Yours alone. O God, from my youth You have taught me, and I still proclaim Your wondrous deeds. So even to old age and gray hairs, O God, do not forsake me, until I proclaim Your might to another generation, Your power to all those to come.
Psalms 71: 15-18

It is here in this section, **Testimony**, that you will record the answers to your prayers as well as any words or promises that God has spoken to you about the things you are praying. There are no jump points for this section because this area is simply for the purpose of recording His marvelous acts.

I have discovered over the years the importance of documenting what God is doing. Many times the Lord answers our prayers, but He does it in such a humble way without great fanfare that we miss it. But beloved, we haven't taken the time to become diligent in our prayer life to simply miss God at the answer stage.

In the **Testimony** section of this journal we make ourselves like the watchman in Habakkuk 2:1 who says this: *I will take my stand at my watch post and station myself on the tower, and look out to see what he will say to me, and what I will answer concerning my complaint.*

In other words, the watchmen is saying this: I've prayed my prayer and now I am going to wait and see what word God speaks to me, *through me*, in answer to my complaint.

Listen to what God's response to the watchmen is: *And the LORD answered me "Write the vision; make it plain on tablets so he may run who reads it. For still the vision awaits its appointed time; it hastens to the end—it will not lie. If it seems slow, wait for it; it will surely come; it will not delay (Habakkuk 2: 2-3).*

> **Many times the Lord answers our prayers but He does it in such a humble way without great fanfare that we miss it.**

God is saying, "Document it, and write it all down, clearly, so that those who come after you with a mind to understand spiritual things can get a running start out of the gate. I have a set, appointed time for your answer to come into the earth. It may feel slow to you, but it's on the 'hurry up' plan—in fact, it might just beat the runner, so you just keep on waiting, keep anticipating, because I'm God, I cannot lie and my word is a sure thing. You can bank on it."

I don't know about you, but that's really good news to me! That Scripture builds my faith. So document, write clearly and plainly. Keep this book long after you fill it up so that it may be a testimony to your posterity. So that your future generations, the ones in your family with a mind and a heart to grow through the power of prayer, will know that you served a God who answers prayer. You did business with Him, and they can too.

MY TESTAMONY

MY TESTAMONY

MY TESTAMONY

MY TESTAMONY

MY TESTAMONY

MY TESTAMONY

MY TESTAMONY

MY TESTAMONY

....
....
....
....
....
....
....
....
....
....
....
....
....

MY TESTAMONY

ABOUT THE AUTHOR

Catrina J. Sparkman is a licensed, ordained minister and the founder of The Ironer's Press Ministries, which host Prayer Parties— a quarterly gathering of intercessors from all over the Midwest, as well as The Fourth Watch— a 3AM-6AM prayer meeting, that happens every Friday morning in her home city of Madison WI. Catrina is a graduate of the University of Wisconsin Madison with a Bachelors of Arts in English, Creative Writing, and graduate work in African American Studies, Theatre and Drama. She is the owner of Abba's Earth Soaps, Natural Handcrafted Soap Company. Trained as a playwright, Sparkman has authored three original stage plays, a radio drama series for children, and one screenplay. She is the recipient of the William F. Vilas award; and works as a content writer, consultant, presenter, and personal empowerment coach, for various church and secular organizations. Catrina lives in Madison, WI with her husband, Wesley, and their three adorable children.

www.ingramcontent.com/pod-product-compliance
Lightning Source LLC
Chambersburg PA
CBHW052142110526
44591CB00012B/1828